ESCAPE

ES-CAPE (verb)
To avoid a threatening evil

WRITTEN BY
MING & WAH

ILLUSTRATED BY
CARMEN VELA

 Lantana

cling SYRIA TO GREECE 2015

dart MEXICO & CENTRAL AMERICA TO UNITED STATES 1986

defy AUSTRIA TO CHINA 1938-1940

disguise SCOTLAND TO FRANCE 1745

flee KIRIBATI TO NEW ZEALAND 2007

fly CZECHOSLOVAKIA TO AUSTRIA 1984

pedal PARIS TO PORTUGAL 1940

raft CUBA TO FLORIDA 1960-1990s

sprint ERITREA TO SUDAN 1981

stowaway SOUTHERN TO NORTHERN UNITED STATES & CANADA 1850-1860

swim CHINA TO HONG KONG 1950s-1970s

tunnel EAST TO WEST GERMANY 1964

SOUTHERN TO NORTHERN UNITED STATES
& CANADA 1850–1860

MEXICO & CENTRAL AMERICA
TO UNITED STATES 1986

CUBA TO FLORIDA 1960–1990s

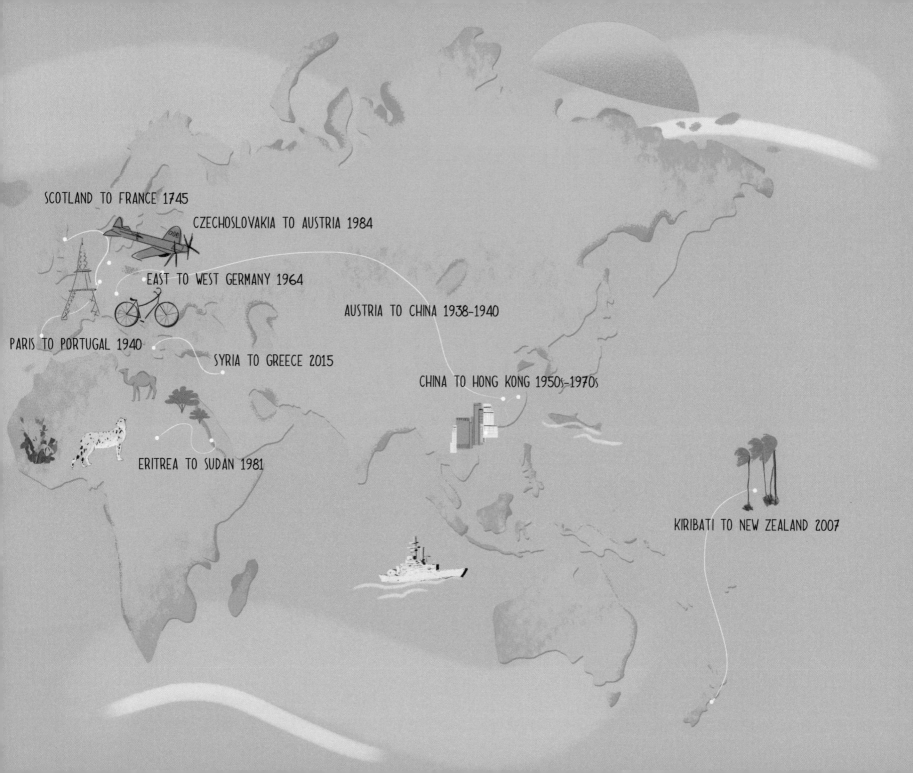

SCOTLAND TO FRANCE 1745

CZECHOSLOVAKIA TO AUSTRIA 1984

EAST TO WEST GERMANY 1964

AUSTRIA TO CHINA 1938-1940

PARIS TO PORTUGAL 1940

SYRIA TO GREECE 2015

CHINA TO HONG KONG 1950s-1970s

ERITREA TO SUDAN 1981

KIRIBATI TO NEW ZEALAND 2007

cling

Fleeing the war-torn city of Damascus in Syria, two sisters, Yusra and Sara Mardini, climbed into an overloaded dinghy in Turkey that was heading for Greece. Not far from a Greek island, the boat's engine died. The two girls jumped into the choppy waters to stop the boat from capsizing. The sisters clung on for hours, shivering with cold, helping direct the dinghy. A larger boat filled with refugees sped past but ignored their cries for help, as did coast guard patrols. The boat's engine eventually sputtered to life and they reached the shore. They made it to Germany, where Yusra competed in the 2016 Rio Summer Olympic Games as a swimmer for the Refugee Olympic Team. Like the sisters, millions of Syrians have been displaced since the Syrian civil war started in 2011.

dart

WILL THEY SEE ME? WILL THEY HEAR ME? WILL I MAKE IT?

Twenty-one year old Laura Alvarez huddled near the U.S.–Mexico border, evading the United States Border Patrol. She had given her life savings to a "coyote," a smuggler, to help her leave her small town in Mexico where violent gangs dominated daily life and jobs were scarce. Believing in the promise of a better life on the other side of the border, she left her family behind and crossed mountains and a highway by foot. Hundreds of thousands of immigrants from Mexico and Central America have risked their lives crossing into New Mexico, Arizona, Texas, or California. Laura made it to Los Angeles, where she was able to work hard as a property manager and raise two fine sons.

defy

GO WITH YOUR GUT. DO WHAT IS RIGHT. DISREGARD ORDERS.

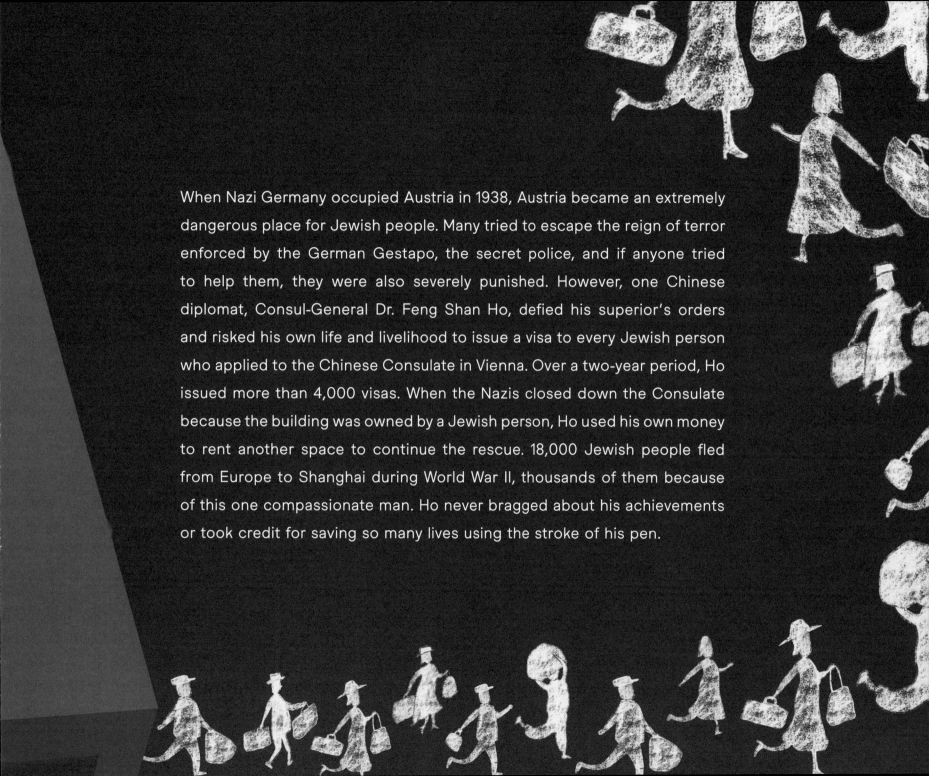

When Nazi Germany occupied Austria in 1938, Austria became an extremely dangerous place for Jewish people. Many tried to escape the reign of terror enforced by the German Gestapo, the secret police, and if anyone tried to help them, they were also severely punished. However, one Chinese diplomat, Consul-General Dr. Feng Shan Ho, defied his superior's orders and risked his own life and livelihood to issue a visa to every Jewish person who applied to the Chinese Consulate in Vienna. Over a two-year period, Ho issued more than 4,000 visas. When the Nazis closed down the Consulate because the building was owned by a Jewish person, Ho used his own money to rent another space to continue the rescue. 18,000 Jewish people fled from Europe to Shanghai during World War II, thousands of them because of this one compassionate man. Ho never bragged about his achievements or took credit for saving so many lives using the stroke of his pen.

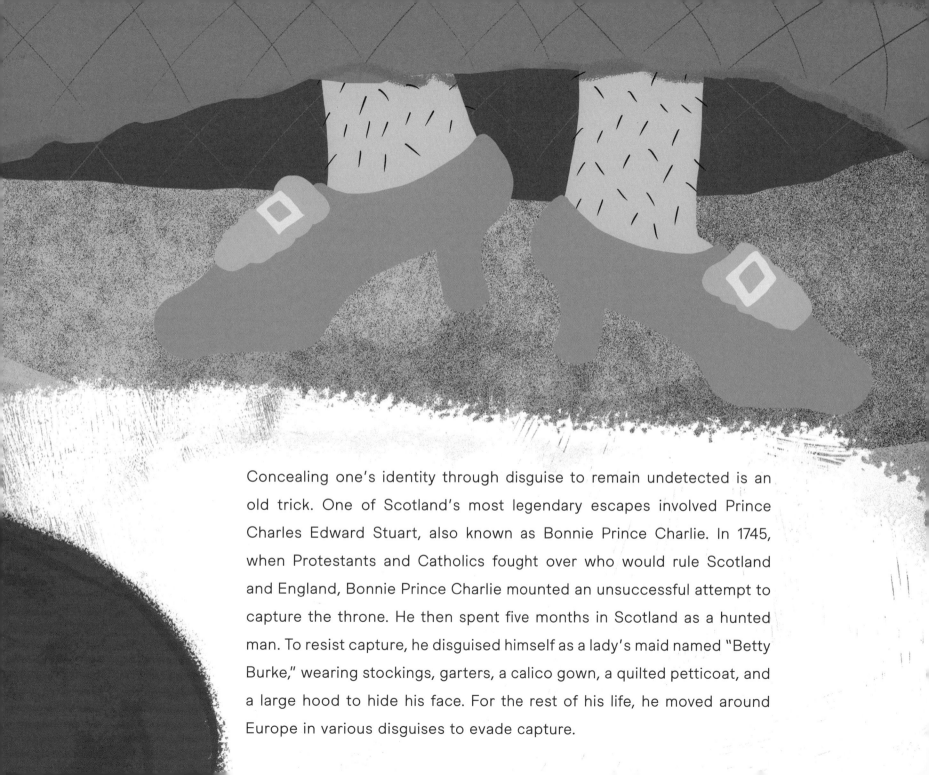

Concealing one's identity through disguise to remain undetected is an old trick. One of Scotland's most legendary escapes involved Prince Charles Edward Stuart, also known as Bonnie Prince Charlie. In 1745, when Protestants and Catholics fought over who would rule Scotland and England, Bonnie Prince Charlie mounted an unsuccessful attempt to capture the throne. He then spent five months in Scotland as a hunted man. To resist capture, he disguised himself as a lady's maid named "Betty Burke," wearing stockings, garters, a calico gown, a quilted petticoat, and a large hood to hide his face. For the rest of his life, he moved around Europe in various disguises to evade capture.

flee

A warming climate is wreaking havoc on the earth, washing away coastlines, and threatening coastal cities and islands. In 2007, Ioane Teitiota left the Pacific Island of Kiribati for New Zealand. He applied for a visa to remain there because rising sea levels were endangering his home country. His case went all the way to New Zealand's Supreme Court but was ultimately rejected. However, New Zealand's Prime Minister, Jacinda Ardern, later proposed a special refugee status, allowing a small number of people fleeing the Pacific Islands due to climate change to live in New Zealand. Ioane became the first legal climate change refugee. Cyclones, tsunamis, droughts, and other extreme weather conditions will continue to displace people from their homes. Forward-thinking nations like New Zealand are at the forefront of preparing for a looming wave of climate refugees.

fly

REV UP.
LIFT OFF. SOAR.

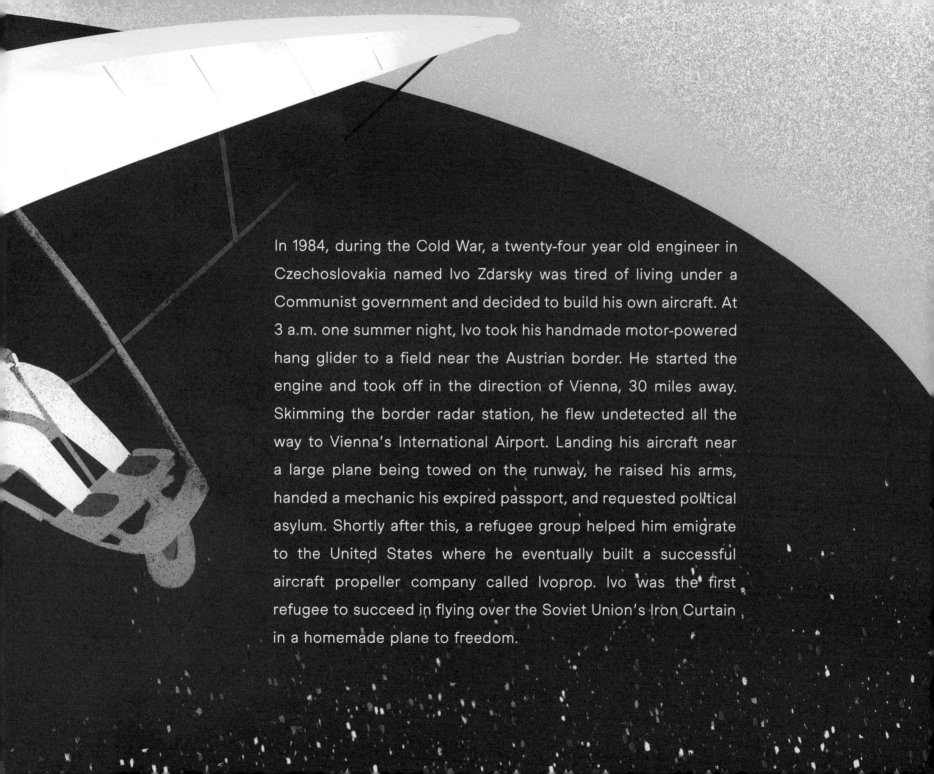

In 1984, during the Cold War, a twenty-four year old engineer in Czechoslovakia named Ivo Zdarsky was tired of living under a Communist government and decided to build his own aircraft. At 3 a.m. one summer night, Ivo took his handmade motor-powered hang glider to a field near the Austrian border. He started the engine and took off in the direction of Vienna, 30 miles away. Skimming the border radar station, he flew undetected all the way to Vienna's International Airport. Landing his aircraft near a large plane being towed on the runway, he raised his arms, handed a mechanic his expired passport, and requested political asylum. Shortly after this, a refugee group helped him emigrate to the United States where he eventually built a successful aircraft propeller company called Ivoprop. Ivo was the first refugee to succeed in flying over the Soviet Union's Iron Curtain in a homemade plane to freedom.

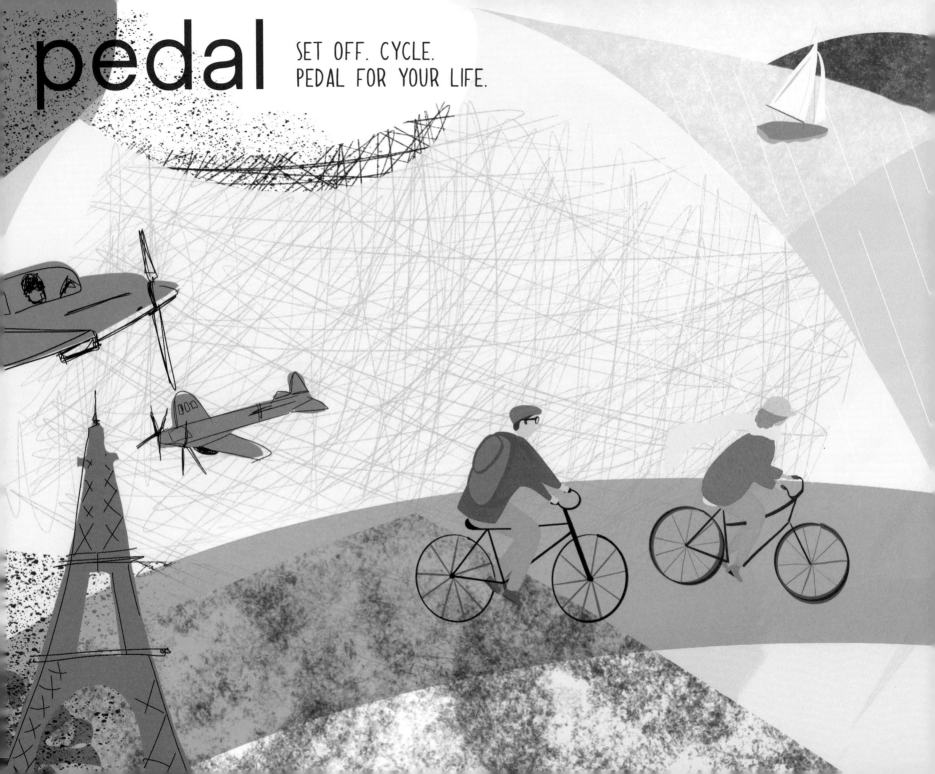

pedal

SET OFF. CYCLE.
PEDAL FOR YOUR LIFE.

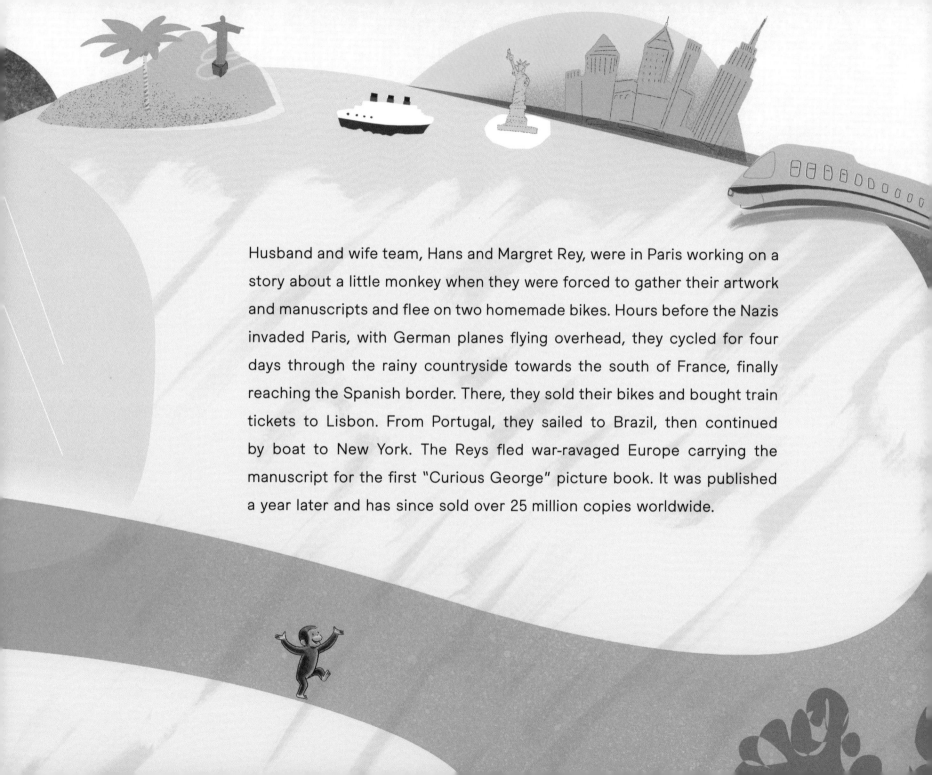

Husband and wife team, Hans and Margret Rey, were in Paris working on a story about a little monkey when they were forced to gather their artwork and manuscripts and flee on two homemade bikes. Hours before the Nazis invaded Paris, with German planes flying overhead, they cycled for four days through the rainy countryside towards the south of France, finally reaching the Spanish border. There, they sold their bikes and bought train tickets to Lisbon. From Portugal, they sailed to Brazil, then continued by boat to New York. The Reys fled war-ravaged Europe carrying the manuscript for the first "Curious George" picture book. It was published a year later and has since sold over 25 million copies worldwide.

raft

Fidel Albelo spent years hoarding materials to build a raft. Bringing only food, water, and rum, and giving the impression they were going fishing, he and his two cousins crept out early one morning, telling no one. People they loved woke up the next day to find them gone. From 1960 to the 1990s, without money or the legal ability to go by plane or boat, thousands of "balseros," Spanish for rafters, used rickety man-made rafts in an attempt to escape Cuba's oppressive dictatorship. Every stage of the journey was dangerous. They struggled to avoid drowning, dehydration, shark attacks, and detection by Cuban or U.S. Coast Guards who sent rafters back to Cuba for immediate imprisonment. However, many people attempted the voyage, racing to touch dry land on American soil for the chance to become U.S. citizens. Albelo made it to Miami and became a well-respected wrestling coach and referee.

His wife made him flee. Russom Keflezighi did not want to leave her and their six children, but he had no choice. Soldiers were killing men during the civil war in Eritrea. For seven days, he walked through chest-high rivers and across plains, dodging wild animals and enemy soldiers, to finally reach Sudan. Once there, he followed other refugees to Italy and worked cleaning offices, sending money back to his family. Five years later, Russom was reunited with his wife and children, and they all resettled in the United States. He had walked the equivalent of ten marathons to leave his home country. Years later, his son Meb Keflezighi became one of America's greatest long-distance runners, winning both the New York and Boston Marathons.

stowaway

RUN AWAY. HIDE.
FOLLOW THE NORTH STAR.

The Underground Railroad was not an actual railroad but a network of secret routes and safe houses in the U.S. fanning out from southern slave states to northern free states, and to Canada where slavery had been abolished. Many slaves stowed away on boats to cross the Ohio River, moving by night in extreme secrecy. Harriet Tubman was one of the many courageous people, some of whom were once slaves themselves, who risked everything—family separation, torture, and death—to help others escape slavery. Harriet made thirteen missions on the Underground Railroad, helping rescue an estimated seventy enslaved people. Slavery was finally abolished in the United States in 1865.

swim

DIVE IN. DON'T THINK. JUST SWIM.

Every night, people left their villages and cities in mainland China to escape famine and the violent upheaval of the Cultural Revolution. Chan Hak-chi and his girlfriend Li Kit-hing made the decision to leave, and they started training every day. Finally, they connected themselves to each other with rope and dived into one of the deep and dirty bays in the southernmost region of mainland China, heading towards British Hong Kong. Even though they took the shortest route, they still had to swim for six hours through shark-infested waters during a typhoon. From the 1950s to the 1970s, more than 700,000 peasants, students, workers, soldiers, and city dwellers fled from China to Hong Kong. Thousands escaped by swimming. An untold number died from exhaustion or drowning; others were attacked by sharks. Many were caught by Chinese gunboat patrols or soldiers and shot or sent back to China. Yet many, like Chan and Li, made it to shore and began a life with freedom, food, and a brighter future.

tunnel

DIG, DIG, UNDER THE WALL.
FASTER, DEEPER. DIG.

In 1961, during the Cold War, the Berlin Wall was erected without warning to separate Soviet-controlled East Germany from West Germany. Many people were desperate to leave the police state of East Germany for the West. Three years later, a small group of students began digging under an unused bakery in West Germany, burrowing a tunnel longer than the length of an American football field to a spot behind an apartment building in East Germany. Among them was a young man named Joachim Neumann, whose girlfriend

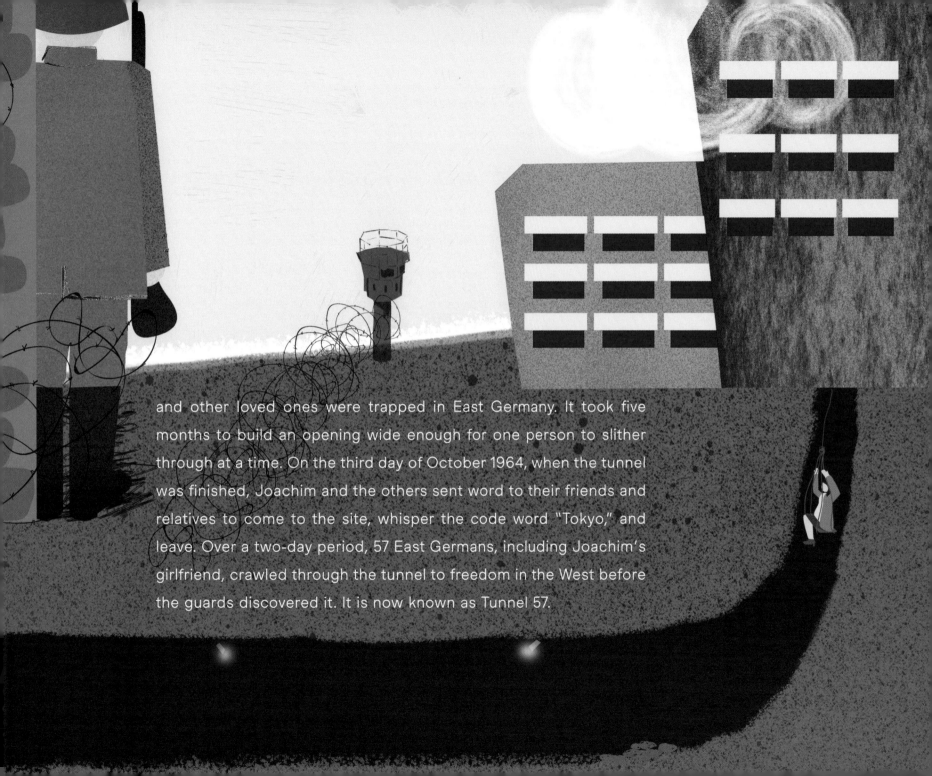

and other loved ones were trapped in East Germany. It took five months to build an opening wide enough for one person to slither through at a time. On the third day of October 1964, when the tunnel was finished, Joachim and the others sent word to their friends and relatives to come to the site, whisper the code word "Tokyo," and leave. Over a two-day period, 57 East Germans, including Joachim's girlfriend, crawled through the tunnel to freedom in the West before the guards discovered it. It is now known as Tunnel 57.

The Universal Declaration of Human Rights

ARTICLE 13.

(1) Everyone has the right to freedom of movement and residence within the borders of each state.

(2) Everyone has the right to leave any country, including his own, and to return to his country.

ARTICLE 14.

(1) Everyone has the right to seek and to enjoy in other countries asylum from persecution.

For more information, visit:
https://www.un.org/en/universal-declaration-human-rights/

"To the cherished grandchildren of Tom
& Margaret Chen: Jacob, Emma, Tyler,
Charlotte, Wyeth, Tommy, Rainey, JT,
Kensi, Oliver, & Parker."

MING & WAH

"To those who leave their
home not by choice but
through an act of strength
and survival."

CARMEN

First published in the United Kingdom in 2021 by Lantana Publishing Ltd., Oxford.
www.lantanapublishing.com | info@lantanapublishing.com

American edition published in 2021 by Lantana Publishing Ltd., UK.
Reprinted in 2021

Text © Ming Chen & Wah Chen, 2021
Illustration © Carmen Vela, 2021

Distributed in the United States and Canada by Lerner Publishing Group, Inc.
241 First Avenue North, Minneapolis, MN 55401 U.S.A.
For reading levels and more information, look for this title at www.lernerbooks.com
Cataloging-in-Publication Data Available.

Printed and bound in the EU.
Original artwork created digitally.

Hardcover ISBN: 978-1-911373-81-0
PDF ISBN: 978-1-911373-85-8
Trade ePub ISBN: 978-1-913747-62-6
S&L ePub ISBN: 978-1-913747-50-3